A JOURNEY INTO
ADAPTATION

WITH MAX AXIOM
SUPER SCIENTIST

by Agnieszka Biskup

illustrated by Cynthia Martin
and Barbara Schulz

Consultant:
Dr. Ronald Browne
Associate Professor of Elementary Education
Minnesota State University, Mankato

Capstone
press

Mankato, Minnesota

Graphic Library is published by Capstone Press,
151 Good Counsel Drive, P.O. Box 669, Mankato, Minnesota 56002.
www.capstonepress.com

1 2 3 4 5 6 12 11 10 09 08 07

Library of Congress Cataloging-in-Publication Data
Biskup, Agnieszka.
  A journey into adaptation with Max Axiom, super scientist / by Agnieszka Biskup; illustrated
by Cynthia Martin and Barbara Schulz.
    p. cm.—Graphic library. Graphic science)
  Summary: "In graphic novel format, follows the adventures of Max Axiom as he explains the
science behind adaptation"—Provided by publisher.
  Includes bibliographical references.
  ISBN-13: 978-0-7368-6840-2 (hardcover)
  ISBN-10: 0-7368-6840-2 (hardcover)
  ISBN-13: 978-0-7368-7892-0 (softcover pbk.)
  ISBN-10: 0-7368-7892-0 (softcover pbk.)
  1. Adaptation (Biology)—Juvenile literature. I. Martin, Cynthia, 1961– ill. II. Schulz,
Barbara Jo, ill. III. Title. IV. Series.
QH546.B57 2007
578.4—dc22   2006031800

Art Director and Designer
Bob Lentz and Thomas Emery

Cover Artist
Tod Smith

Colorist
Michael Kelleher

Editor
Christopher L. Harbo

Photo illustration credits: Charles Darwin Research Station, 8; Corbis/Dan Guravich, 25;
Corbis/Joe McDonald, 7; Corbis/Kevin Schafer, 14

TABLE of CONTENTS

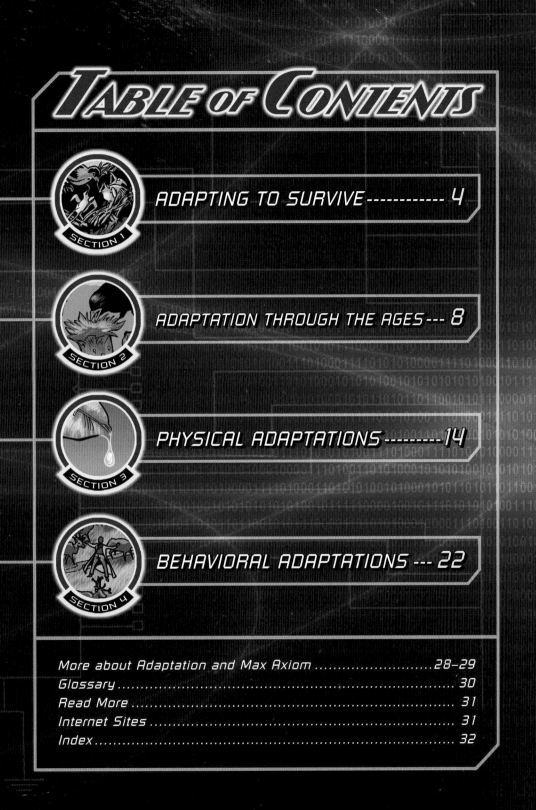

Using bushes for cover, Super Scientist Max Axiom begins his adventures in adaptation from his own backyard.

I'm always amazed by the wonders of nature.

For the animals that live here, my backyard serves as their habitat.

It provides the food, water, and shelter they need to survive.

But wings are not this hawk's only adaptation. Its feathers also help it fly and stay warm.

Its excellent eyesight, sharp claws, and curved beak help the hawk catch and kill the small animals it eats.

Together, all of these adaptations help the hawk survive in its habitat.

FLYING SQUIRREL

ACCESS GRANTED: MAX AXIOM

It's a bird! It's a plane! It's a squirrel? The flying squirrel has a fold of skin connecting the wrists of its front legs to the ankles of its back legs. This fold of skin helps the squirrel glide from tree branch to tree branch. With a good jump, flying squirrels can glide 20 to 30 feet through the air.

The large ground finch, for example, has a strong beak that works like a nutcracker. It's adapted to crack big, hard seeds.
GROUND FINCH
The cactus finch has a beak that works like a pair of needle-nose pliers. It's just the right shape to dig into cactus plants.
CACTUS FINCH
WARBLER FINCH
The warbler finch has a beak like a pair of tweezers. Its beak is adapted to probe into small cracks to catch insects.
In all cases, the finches have beaks that help them survive on the island where they live.
But what if a finch with a seed-crushing bill got stuck on a rocky island without seeds?
Would it survive?

Actually, most animals need many generations to adapt to their environments. Rapid changes in an environment make survival very difficult.

The dinosaurs found this out the hard way 65 million years ago.

The meteorite's impact threw huge amounts of dust and ash into the air. This debris blocked out the sun's light and temperatures fell.

KA-BOOM!

Why did the dinosaurs go extinct? No one knows for sure. But some scientists believe that the climate changed quickly after a meteorite the size of a mountain hit earth.

With less sunlight and colder temperatures, plants began to die.

The dinosaurs that ate those plants now had less to eat. As the plant-eating dinosaurs died, the meat-eaters also lost their food source.

The dinosaurs couldn't adapt to these sudden changes and died.

Clearly, being able to adapt really is a matter of life and death.

CIMOLESTES

Many reptiles, mammals, and insects did adapt to earth's changing climate 65 million years ago. One such animal was called cimolestes. This shrewlike mammal fed on insects and worms. It survived several million years after the dinosaurs died out.

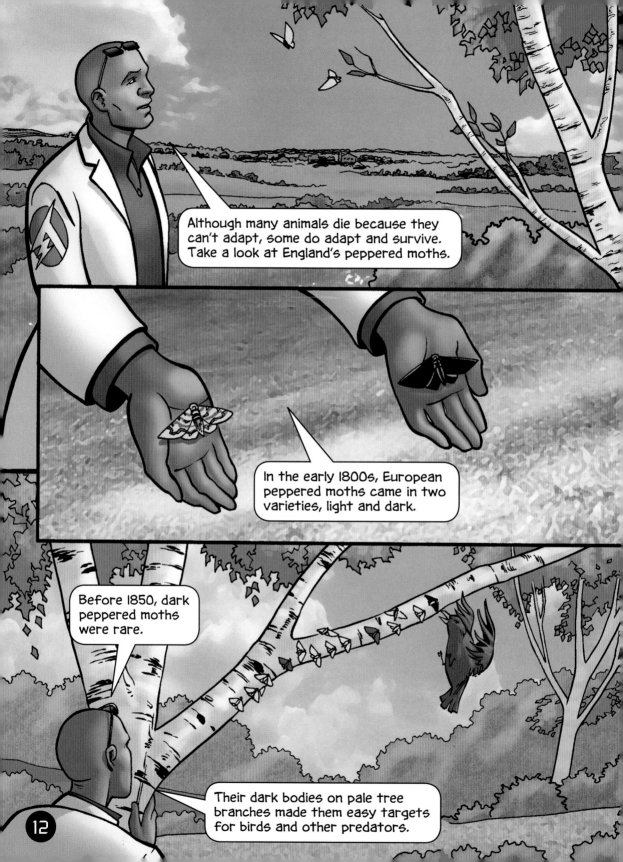

Although many animals die because they can't adapt, some do adapt and survive. Take a look at England's peppered moths.

In the early 1800s, European peppered moths came in two varieties, light and dark.

Before 1850, dark peppered moths were rare.

Their dark bodies on pale tree branches made them easy targets for birds and other predators.

By the late 1800s, England had a huge increase in factories. Those factories spewed soot and smoke into the air. Before long, the bark of the trees became dirty and blackened.

Now the light peppered moths became easy to see.

They were the ones the predators found and ate.

Eventually, more dark moths survived to produce dark-colored offspring. The population of moths became mostly dark-colored.

The peppered moth had adapted to its changing environment.

The body features, or physical adaptations, of plants and animals often relate to the environments they live in.

For example, a camel's hump is an adaptation for desert life. When food and water are scarce, the camel uses fat stored in its hump for energy.

The camel's long eyelashes and fuzzy ear hair protect its eyes and ears from blowing sand.

CREOSOTE BUSH

Plants also cope with dry desert conditions. Since plants lose water through their leaves, the creosote bush has adapted. Its leaves have a waxy coating to help the plant hold in water.

BARREL CACTUS

In many cases, plants lack leaves altogether. The barrel cactus stores water in its fleshy stem.

FENNEC FOX

ACCESS GRANTED: MAX AXIOM

Is fur a good adaptation for the desert? For the fennec fox it is. This fox's fur keeps it warm at night when the desert is cold. During the day, the light colored fur reflects sunlight to help keep the fox cool.

Hi, Dr. Diaz. What are you studying today?

But what about places like rain forests that are hot and very wet? How do living things adapt to these conditions?

I know a biologist just ahead who studies rain forest plant life. I bet he sees adaptations every day.

Hello, Max. I'm glad you found me. I'm taking samples of this philodendron plant.

Wow, this leaf feels waxy. Back in the desert, some plants had waxy leaves to hold in water.

That's true, but the waxy coating has a different purpose in the rain forest. It helps plants repel extra water like a raincoat.

In fact, many rain forest plants also have drip tips to help them shed water. These features prevent the growth of bacteria and fungi on the plants.

DRIP TIP

BBRRRAOOOOOMM!!

Just like they do underwater, people need extra gear to survive when it's cold outside. But arctic animals have adapted to their cold climate.

What a beautiful arctic fox, Dr. Ling. It must be a real survivor to live in this frigid climate.

You're right, Max. The freezing temperatures here can be deadly.

Like many arctic animals, this fox has thick fur. Its small ears and compact body keep it from losing too much body heat.

YIP! YIP!

Well, Max, it's time for this little guy to return to the wild.

And the hair under its paws keeps its feet from sinking into the snow, kind of like snowshoes.

Sounds good. I need to head out as well. Thanks for the information, Dr. Ling.

17

Sometimes, the best way to survive is to stay out of sight.

Camouflage is an adaptation some animals use to avoid being eaten by predators.

The arctic hare, for example, has a white fur coat to match the snow.

But when spring rolls around, its fur starts turning brown to match the emerging ground.

Camouflage even helps young fawns. Their spotted coats hide them in the light and dark shadows of the forest.

Adaptations are not only about physical features. The way animals behave helps them survive too.

For instance, a porcupine thrusts out its quills when it feels threatened.

YELP!

The hognose snake becomes a great actor when threatened. First it pretends to twist with pain. Then it turns upside down, throws back its head, opens its mouth, and sticks out its tongue.

Why does it behave this way? It plays dead because most predators prefer to catch their prey alive.

Along with predators, animals also face harsh conditions in their habitats.

Mice, squirrels, skunks, and bears live in areas where food is scarce during long winters. To survive they hibernate.

During hibernation, animals go into what appears to be a deep sleep.

SUBJECT:
HIBERNATION

Animals that hibernate slow down their body functions. Their heart and breathing rates slow. They don't eat for weeks or months. They live on fat stored in the body.

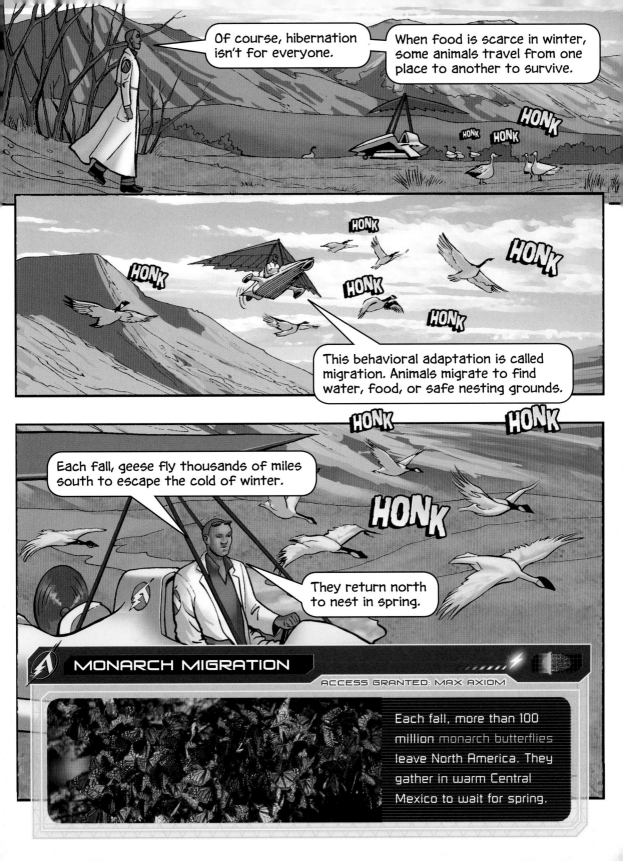

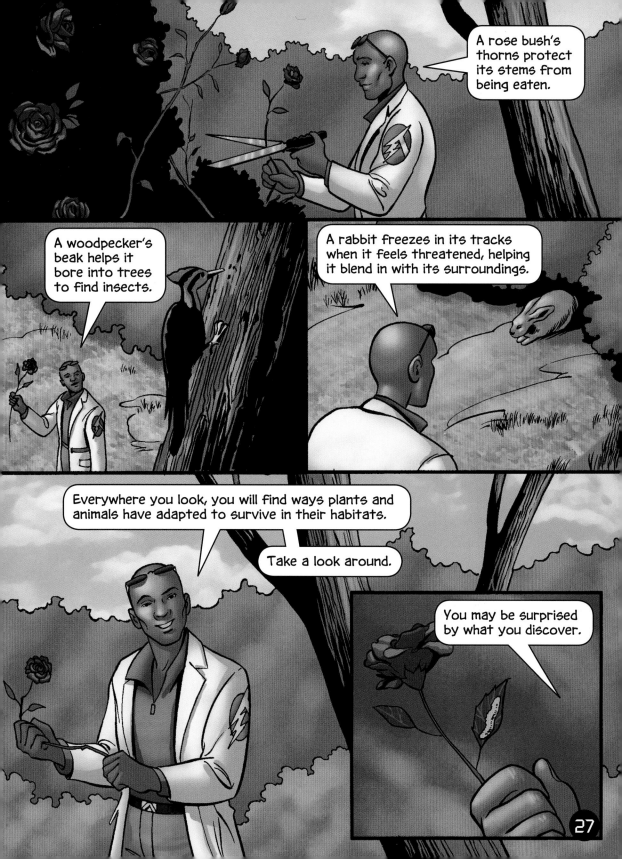

MORE ABOUT ADAPTATION

Not all flowers smell sweet. In fact, the flowers of the rafflesia plant have adapted to smell just like rotten meat. They give off the horrible smell to attract flies. The flies then carry the rafflesia's pollen to other flowers.

The mimic octopus is a master of mimicry. By changing its shape and color, it can look like sole fish, sea snakes, or lionfish. Scientists believe the octopus developed its mimicry skills because its normal habitat doesn't allow it many places to hide from predators.

Some tube worms, crabs, and clams live at the bottom of the ocean without sunlight or plant life. These animals have adapted to feed on bacteria that grow on the sulfur-rich chemicals spewing from active underwater volcanoes.

Keeping clean is an important behavioral adaptation. Many animals increase their chances for survival by grooming themselves and each other. Monkeys comb through each other's fur, picking off dirt and bugs that might spread disease. Birds preen their feathers to remove bugs and to keep their feathers in first-rate shape for flight.

The Venus flytrap is famous for its ability to trap and digest insects that land on its leaves. This carnivorous plant has adapted to eat insects because the poor soil it lives in doesn't provide enough nutrients.

 Bald rockcod have adapted to the freezing temperatures in the Antarctic Ocean. These fish have chemicals in their bodies that work just like antifreeze does in a car. The chemicals keep the fish from freezing solid in the frigid water below the Antarctic ice shelves.

The North American wood frog has adapted to arctic winters by using an extreme form of hibernation. In winter, the frog goes into a deep sleep. Its heartbeat and breathing slow to a stop. Amazingly, much of its body freezes solid. In spring, the wood frog's body thaws and its breathing and heartbeat restart.

MORE ABOUT

MAX AXIOM
SUPER SCIENTIST

Real name: Maxwell J. Axiom
Hometown: Seattle, Washington
Height: 6' 1"   **Weight:** 192 lbs
Eyes: Brown   **Hair:** None

Super capabilities: Super intelligence; able to shrink to the size of an atom; sunglasses give x-ray vision; lab coat allows for travel through time and space.

Origin: Since birth, Max Axiom seemed destined for greatness. His mother, a marine biologist, taught her son about the mysteries of the sea. His father, a nuclear physicist and volunteer park ranger, schooled Max on the wonders of earth and sky.

One day on a wilderness hike, a megacharged lightning bolt struck Max with blinding fury. When he awoke, Max discovered a newfound energy and set out to learn as much about science as possible. He traveled the globe earning degrees in every aspect of the field. Upon his return, he was ready to share his knowledge and new identity with the world. He had become Max Axiom, Super Scientist.

GLOSSARY

bacteria (bak-TIHR-ee-uh)—very small living things; some bacteria cause disease.

camouflage (KAM-uh-flahzh)—coloring or covering that makes animals, people, and objects look like their surroundings

carnivorous (kar-NIV-ur-uhss)—to eat meat; the Venus flytrap is one type of carnivorous plant.

climate (KLYE-mit)—the usual weather in a place

extinct (ek-STINGKT)—no longer living anywhere in the world

generation (jen-uh-RAY-shuhn)—the average amount of time between the birth of parents and that of their offspring

habitat (HAB-uh-tat)—the place and natural conditions where an animal lives

hibernate (HYE-bur-nate)—to spend winter in a deep sleep

migration (mye-GRAY-shuhn)—the regular movement of animals as they search different places for food

mimic (MIM-ik)—to copy the look, actions, or behaviors of another plant or animal

predator (PRED-uh-tur)—an animal that hunts and eats other animals

prey (PRAY)—an animal hunted by another animal for food

reproduce (ree-pruh-DOOSE)—to breed and have offspring

specimen (SPESS-uh-muhn)—a sample that a scientist studies closely

READ MORE

Burton, Jane. *The Nature and Science of Survival.* Exploring the Science of Nature. Milwaukee: Gareth Stevens, 2001.

Goodman, Susan E. *Claws, Coats, and Camouflage: The Ways Animals Fit into Their World.* Brookfield, Conn.: Millbrook Press, 2001.

Knight, Tim. *Super Survivors.* Amazing Nature. Chicago: Heinemann Library, 2003.

Parker, Steve. *Adaptation.* Life Processes. Chicago: Heinemann Library, 2006.

Taylor, Barbara. *Survival: Life in Earth's Toughest Habitats.* DK Secret Worlds. New York: DK, 2002.

INTERNET SITES

FactHound offers a safe, fun way to find Internet sites related to this book. All of the sites on FactHound have been researched by our staff.

Here's how:
1. Visit *www.facthound.com*
2. Choose your grade level.
3. Type in this book ID **0736868402** for age-appropriate sites. You may also browse subjects by clicking on letters, or by clicking on pictures and words.
4. Click on the **Fetch It** button.

FactHound will fetch the best sites for you!